THE TOMATO
AND OTHER FRUIT VEGETABLES
MILLICENT E. SELSAM
PHOTOGRAPHS BY JEROME WEXLER

WILLIAM MORROW AND COMPANY · NEW YORK

The author and photographer thank
DR. HOWARD S. IRWIN,
Head Curator of the New York Botanical Gardens,
for checking the text and photographs of this book.

ACKNOWLEDGMENTS FOR PHOTOGRAPHS
Grant Haist, National Audubon Society, 47
R. L. House, National Audubon Society, 11
Millicent E. Selsam, 22
Hugh Spencer, National Audubon Society, 46
United States Department of Agriculture, 10, 34, 36 right, 37, 45

If you want to find out
where tomatoes come from,
plant a tomato seed.

A tomato seed
is sprouting.

Two thick fleshy leaves
called seed leaves, or cotyledons,
are pulled out of the seed.
They are full of stored food.
The young plant
uses this food as it grows.

This tomato plant is a type called Tiny Tim.

8   It grows to its full height in a flowerpot.

This tomato plant,
which has been pulled
out of the ground,
is a type
called Big Boy.
It grows more than
six feet in height.

Tomatoes usually are grown outside
in the ground. The stems are weak.
10   They are allowed to spread over the ground.

The leaves are compound,
that is, divided into a number of leaflets.
There are six leaflets in this picture.

There are seven leaflets in this one.
The number varies.

Some flower buds appear.

The flowers are yellow.

In the center of the flower
are the most important parts:
the stamens and the pistil.
They are necessary for making seeds and fruits.   15

PETALS

STAMENS

STAMENS

The flowers usually hang down.
But in these pictures
the petals have been removed
and the flower is being held upright.
You can see the stamens
united into a tube
in the center of the flower.
On their inner side,
they bear sacs of pollen.

If you remove a few stamens,
you can see the pistil inside.

The stigma is at the top.
The style connects the stigma
to the ovary below.
Inside the ovary,
you can see the ovules
that later become seeds.

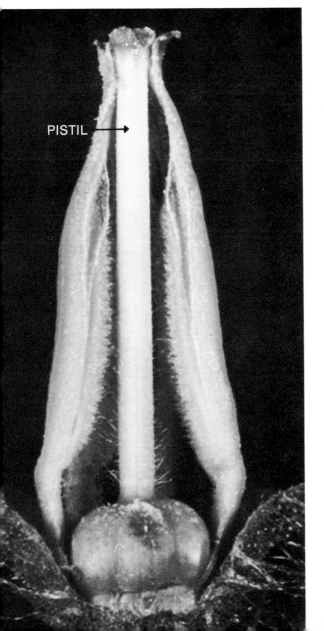
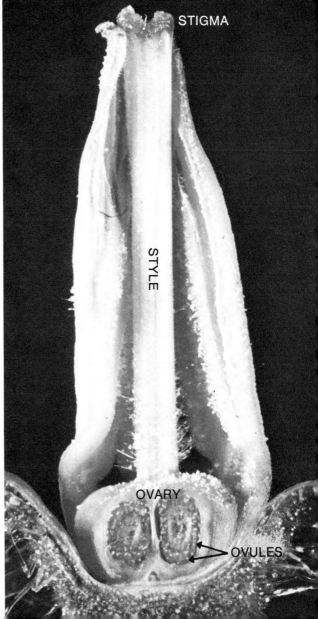

PISTIL

STIGMA

STYLE

OVARY

OVULES

SPLIT
STARTING
HERE

There will be
no tomatoes on this plant
unless pollen
from the stamens
falls on the stigma
of the pistil.
When the petals
are wide open,
the pollen is discharged.
The stamens split open,
and pollen falls
on the stigma
in the center
of the flower.
You can see
the sacs of pollen
starting to split open
at the top.

When the pollen
gets to the stigma,
pollination has taken place.
In the tomato, the pollen
usually falls on the stigma
of the same flower.
This process is called
self-pollination.
If pollen comes from the flowers
of other tomato plants,
the process is called
cross-pollination.
There are many pollen grains.
Each pollen grain
puts out its own tube,
which grows down
through the style
into the ovary.

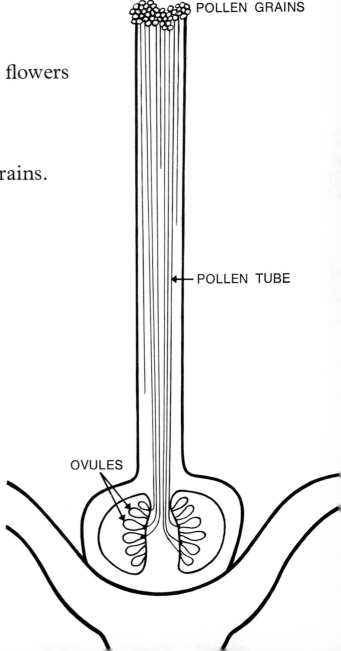

POLLEN GRAINS

POLLEN TUBE

OVULES

When the pollen tubes reach the ovules,
the contents of each one join with each ovule.
This process is called fertilization.
Now the ovules will become seeds,
and the ovary will become a tomato fruit.
Any part of a plant that contains seeds is a fruit.

20

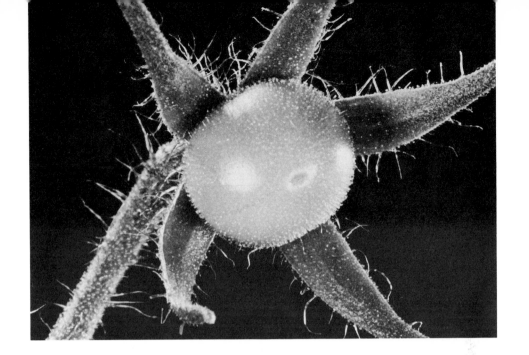

The ovary grows bigger and bigger.

22   The green tomatoes turn red.

In the picture below you can see
a Tiny Tim tomato fruit
next to a Big Boy fruit.

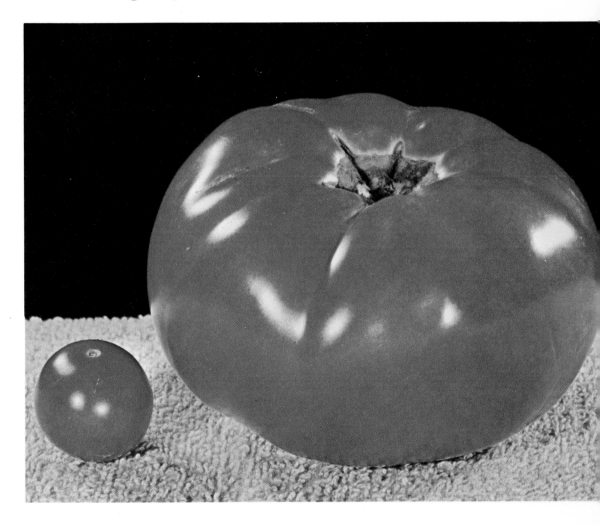

Cut across the tomato,
and you can see the seeds
that have developed from the ovules.
Inside the seeds are tiny little embryos,
ready to grow into new tomato plants.

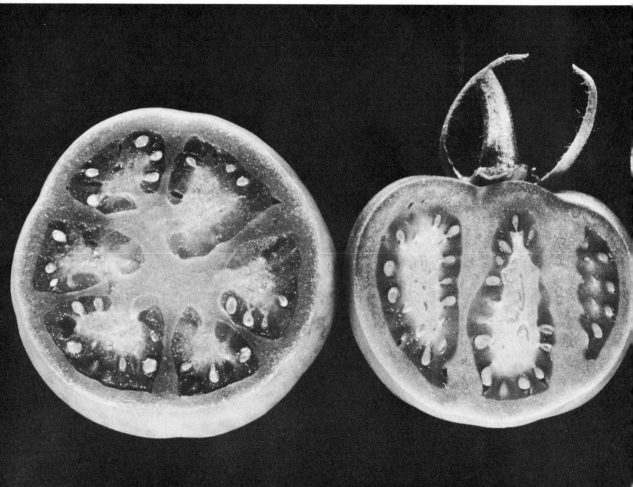

Snap beans are fruits too,
because they are the parts
that contain the seeds of the bean plant.
The bean pod is open to show the seeds.
It, too, grows from the flower's ovary,
which contains the ovules.   25

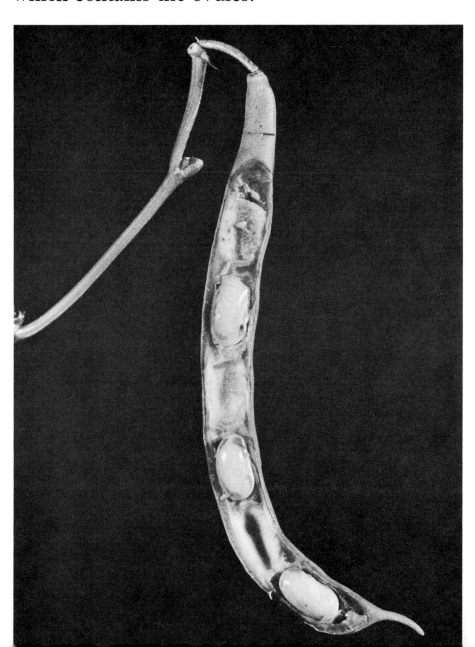

In this picture
a bean seed
is sprouting.

Leaves form.

The plant grows bigger.

Flowers form.

The pollination of the snap bean
is like that of the tomato.
The pollen falls on the stigma of the same flower.
28   The flower is self-pollinated.

After the pollen tubes grow down
to the ovary and fertilize the ovules,
the petals and stamens fall off
and the ovary begins to grow.   29

30 The ovary has become a full-grown bean pod.

Inside the pod are the seeds
that will grow into new bean plants.

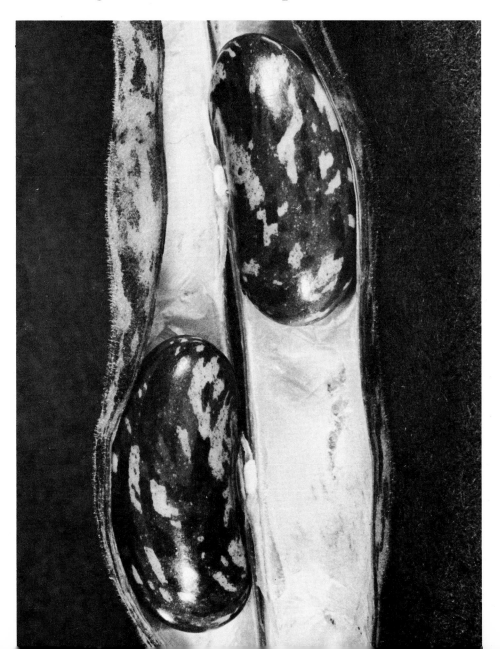

The cucumber comes from the ovary of the flower.
It, too, is a fruit. Find the seeds.

A cucumber seed is sprouting.

Leaves and flowers form.

But there are two different kinds
of flowers on the same plant.
One kind has only stamens.

34

The other kind has the pistil.
Here you can see the ovary below the petals.
Insects take the pollen from one flower to another.

OVARY

After pollination and fertilization,
36   the ovary begins to grow bigger and bigger.

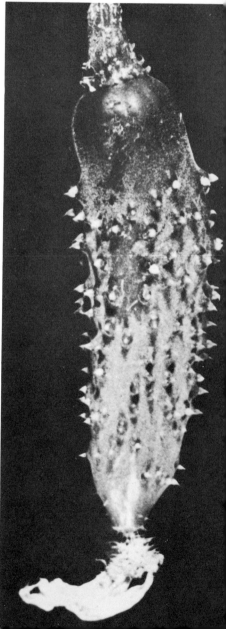

Soon it is
a full-grown
cucumber
with seeds inside.

An eggplant is also a fruit.
It, too, comes from the ovary
of the flower and has seeds inside.

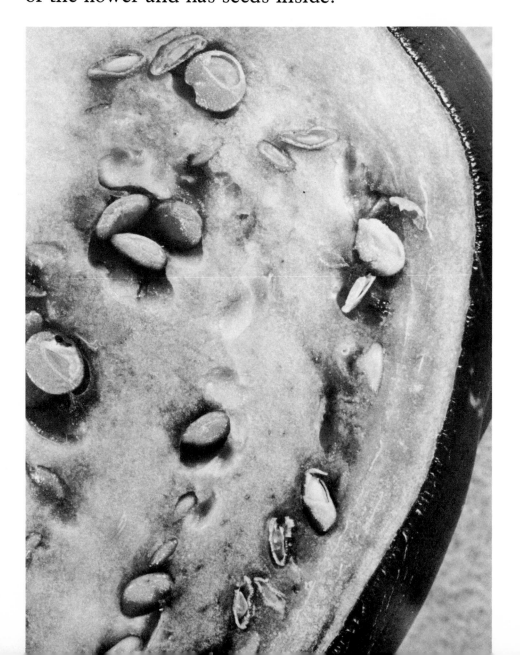

An eggplant seed
is sprouting.

Leaves form.

40   Flowers form. They resemble tomato flowers.

With petals pulled away,
you can see the stamens and the pistil.

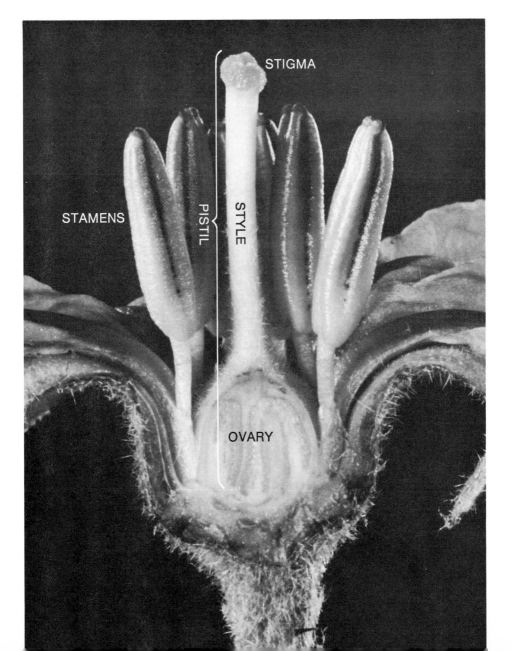

Usually the flower is self-pollinated,
but insects also carry pollen
from one flower to another.

Then the ovary starts to grow.
It gets bigger and bigger.

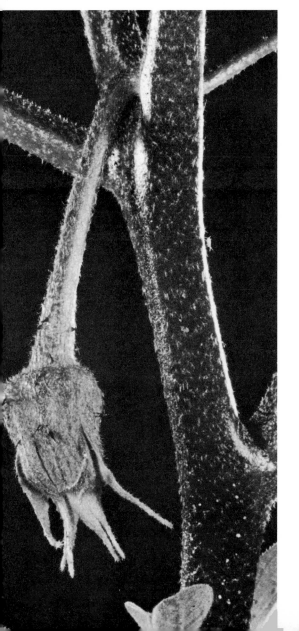

44 Finally you can recognize it as an eggplant.

Can you think of other vegetables
that are really fruits
because they contain seeds?

ABOUT THE AUTHOR

Millicent E. Selsam's career has been closely connected with biology and botany. She majored in biology and was graduated, *magna cum laude* with a B.A. degree from Brooklyn College. At Columbia she received her M.A. in the Department of Botany, and since then has passed all course requirements and a comprehensive examination for a Ph.D., also at Columbia. After teaching biology for ten years in the New York City high schools, she has devoted herself to writing science books for children. Mrs. Selsam and her husband live in New York City and spend their summers on Fire Island, New York.

ABOUT THE PHOTOGRAPHER

Jerome Wexler was born in New York City, where he attended Pratt Institute. Later he studied at the University of Connecticut. His interest in photography started when he was in the ninth grade. After service in World War II, he worked for the State Department in Europe as a photographer. Returning to the United States, he specialized in photographing advanced farming techniques, and the pictures he made have been published throughout the world. When he first became interested in nature photography, he could not find equipment suited to his needs, so he designed and built his own with which he can photograph living plants and insects ten times their life size. Mr. Wexler lives, with his wife and two children, in Yalesville, Connecticut.